KLM
Schiphol Amsterdam
stop

Schiphol

KLM
asia
PH-BFH
KLM
KLM
KLM
PH-KCF

Amsterdam Schiphol Airport is one of the largest and most modern airports in Europe. Passengers here have the choice of 80 airlines and 225 destinations. Below, a view from the esplanade which is open to visitors. Middle left, you can see the entrance of Schiphol Plaza under which the railway station is situated. The airport lies about five metres below sea level. The middle right photo shows the Amsterdam ArenA, pride of many Amsterdammers and home ground of Ajax football club. The roof of the stadium can be opened and closed. This design is to enable the ArenA to be used for all kinds of manifestations. On weekdays, when the complex is not being used, you can park there and take the Metro into the centre of Amsterdam: it's easy, quick and cheap. The Dutch are proud of their sporting heroes and their national colour-orange. As football fever grows in the Netherlands, the country becomes more and more orange. The top right photo shows Rembrandtplein in Amsterdam, where crowds of supporters are gathered before a match.

Amsterdam, the Central Station of the Dutch Railways (NS). The monumental facade dates from 1889. The foundations consist of 8,687 wooden piles (tree trunks). The main entrance of the station leads to the city centre, while the back looks out on the 'IJ', a waterway running eastward to the IJsselmeer. In 1876, digging commenced for the Noordzeekanaal (North Sea Canal), which forms a connection with the North Sea. There is a traditional Dutch coffee house in the beautiful white building directly opposite the main entrance to the station. The Tourist Information Office (VVV) can also be found here. Every five years Amsterdam hosts a magnificent spectacle known as 'Parade of Sail'. All kinds of historical ships from around the world 'parade' along the IJ. This event lasts for one week and during that time swarms of sightseeing and pleasure boats weave their way between the impressive ships. On the photo to the left, the replica of the VOC ship 'Amsterdam' proudly dominating the harbour.

Damplein is the main and definitely the liveliest square in Amsterdam. It connects the Damrak with the Rokin. The Royal Palace on Damplein was built as a town hall in 1648. The imposing building with its neo-classic facade rests on 13,059 wooden piles, many of which had to be imported. The town hall was converted into a palace in 1808 during the short rule of Louis Bonaparte, the brother of Napoleon I. The front and back of the palace are adorned with sculptures by Artus Quellin from Antwerp. The National Monument on the Dam is the liberation monument for the Netherlands, in remembrance of all who fell during the Second World War. It was completed in 1956. Since then, a memorial service is held every year at 20.00 hours on 4 May, the eve of Liberation Day. Prior to two minutes silence, wreathes are laid by Her Majesty the Queen, representatives of the government, and many others. This sea of flowers can be seen on the upper right photo. Behind the monument, the famous Krasnapolski Hotel.

Westertower

Photo left, the Oude Kerk on Oudezijds Voorburgwal dates from the 14th century. As the name rightly implies, this is the oldest church in Amsterdam. Originally (1306) it was a small church in the form of a rose. Towards the end of the following century, many adaptations and extensions were made. The clock tower, from 1565, is 68 m high. The carillon with its 47 bells was designed by François Hemony and is one of the finest in the Netherlands. One of Rembrandt's wives, Saskia, is buried here. In the direct vicinity of the Oude Kerk, Amsterdam's narrowest streets can be found. Photo right: the Oude Schans with the Montelbaanstoren, which was built in 1512, as seen from the bridge on Prins Hendrikkade. When first built, the tower was not so high or imposing as it is now; the spire was added much later in 1606. The Oude Schans is one of the widest of the city's canals and runs into the Oosterdok, and then the IJ, close to the NewMetropolis. This museum is a science and technology centre, designed by the Italian architect Renzo Piano. The Herengracht, photo lower left, is one of the main concentric canals, where wealthy merchants came to live in the 17th century. It's difficult to say which of the houses has the most beautiful gable, numbers 364, 386 to 394, 475 and 502 are especially worth looking at.

Reederij P. Kooy

HARMINA

Behind the Round Lutheran Church on the Singel, two houses on the street Kattegat are worth a mention, the Gouden and Zilveren Spiegel (Golden and Silver Mirror), top left. For many years now, these handsome step-roofed buildings house a fashionable restaurant. What is not so well known is that a Jewish family was hidden here during the Second World War. The owners at that time were Austrians, and German soldiers were regular guests. This is one of the reasons why the secret has been kept better than that of the universally known Anne Frank's house at Prinsengracht 263, lower left. A very unusual feature of the Round Lutheran Church is that the roof, which covers the full width of the church, is also the tower. Permission was given to build the church on the condition that it had no tower. The Lutherans were very crafty and built the church with the whole roof as one big tower. Lower right, the stately canal-side houses on the Singel by the Wijde Heisteeg.

A flower market is held daily on the Singel between the Munttoren and Koningsplein. You can find a wealth of different plants, flowers and seeds here, and between June and January, many different types of tulip bulbs are also on sale. Barges supply the stalls in this very picturesque market. Some of them are actually on the barges, transforming them into floating greenhouses. You will also find souvenir shops with a wide range of goods. Reguliersbreestraat runs from the Munttoren to Rembrandtplein, lower right photos. Here you will find the statue of the most famous Dutch painter Rembrandt van Rijn (Leiden 1606 - Amsterdam 1669). The Stopera concert hall, upper right photo, on the River Amstel dates from 1986 and is a work of the architect Holzbauer. It is the home base of the National Opera and Ballet Company. The concert hall was built as a 'two in one' at the same time as the new town hall. The town hall can be seen in the background to the left with the Stopera dominating to the right.

PEPSI
Rembrandt Bar
RESTAURANT

The Rijksmuseum (National Museum), which dates from 1885, was built in a neo-classic style by the architect P.J.H. Cuypers, top left photo. The museum is especially well known because it houses the world's largest collection of paintings from the 15th and 17th centuries. At the back of the monumental building, in stone relief, Rembrandt can be seen working on his masterpiece 'The Sampling Officials'. His most famous work the 'Night Watch', from 1642, is found in this museum. The Van Gogh Museum with its 200 paintings and 500 drawings from the painter Vincent van Gogh can be seen in the top right photo. The collection includes the sombre paintings of the province of Drenthe (1881-1883), and those from Nuenen (1883-1885). After a stay in Antwerp, Van Gogh moved to Rue Lepic in Paris (1886-1888). You can see self-portraits performed with the help of a mirror, the Bridge of Langlois, and the Yellow

house in Arles. On 27 July 1890, Van Gogh attempted suicide. He died two days later in Auvers-sur-Oise. Opened in 1973, the museum is a work of art by the famous Utrecht architect Gerrit Rietveld. The Concert Hall, dating from 1888, is situated on Van Baerlestraat. The photos to the right show the exterior and the interior during a concert. Further photos below from left to right show the Stadsschouwburg (National Theatre) and the Zuiderkerk, which was built between 1603 and 1611 from a design by the ever-present Hendrik de Keyzer. It was the first protestant church to be rebuilt as a new church after the reformation. The building has not functioned as a church since 1929. And finally, the Westerkerk, which dates from 1620, and is situated at Prinsengracht 279 (close to Anne Frank's house at no. 263). The 85-metre high tower carries the crown of Maximilian of Austria. A memorial shield can be found in this church as the painter Rembrandt van Rijn is buried here.

Durgerdam

Marken

Marken used to be an island, but in 1959 a dam was built which connected it with the mainland. Although this pretty village is not as well known as Volendam, you should not miss it when visiting the Netherlands. There is parking space outside the village where you must leave your car. Then you can enjoy yourself walking around this delightful village, with its quaint wooden houses, little bridges and beautiful gardens. Marken is a living monument, not a museum, and it is just as it was hundreds of years ago. Houses used to be built on wooden piles so that the living quarters were raised above the ground. This construction served as protection against flooding. Outside the village, several groups of houses can be found, built on man-made hills for the same reason. After the completion of the 32 km long 'Afsluitdijk' (IJsselmeer dam) flooding was no longer a problem. If you need a film for your camera, you can always buy one at Sijtje Boes' souvenir shop on the harbour, where they will be happy to supply you with anything you need.

Volendam, one of the most visited tourist spots in the Netherlands. It is an old fishing village and all kinds of fishing boats and yachts can still be found in its harbour. Tons of eels are sold in its famous fish auction. Along the harbour there are shops that sell delicious smoked eel, which together with caviar and salmon make the most exquisite dishes. Why not try them yourself? The traditional costumes of Volendam are looked upon as the most colourful and prettiest in the Netherlands, but unfortunately the younger generations do not wear them very often. The best time to see them is on Sunday morning as the women go to church. If you cannot manage a visit on a Sunday, you still find ladies in their costumes in several shops. The beauty in the photo to the left has hers at Haven 138. You can buy gifts at very reasonable prices in all the shops here. From this very harbour you can take a round trip to Marken, sailing across the former Zuider Sea.

Nicole 3

Katwoude, Volendam

It was in the 12th century that the first dykes were built in the Netherlands, and the first windmills to drain the marshes date from the 14th century. In the 17th century, large lakes were pumped dry to make polders. Polders are pieces of land that are reclaimed from the water. In the province of Noord Holland, Beemster Lake was the first to be reclaimed (1612), followed by Purmer Lake, and the Schermer was pumped dry in 1635. Fifty windmills were built for this purpose, sometimes in rows so that enough water could be pumped up. Two of the three mills built in a row in **Schermerhorn** can be seen in the upper left photo. The middle one is open to the public. The enormous Haarlemmermeer-polder was not completed until 1852. On these pages, going clockwise, you can also see **Monnickendam**, a little old harbour town on the IJsselmeer, which used to be famous for its eels. The Waag (weighing house), dating from around 1600 with its sculpted facade can be seen on the photo. It now contains a restaurant. The 16th century clock tower rises imposingly above the town. Lower left, **Graft's** old town hall, dating from 1613. The hydraulic engineer, Leeghwater (1575-1650), was born in this village; he was an expert in the reclamation of land. A number of cheesemakers and clog-makers can be found in this area, among them the ones in **Katwoude**, where you can see this old trade being carried out according to traditional methods.

This and the following pages are devoted to the **Zaanse Schans**, a museum village on the River Zaan, just north of Amsterdam. The word 'Schans' means rampart. In 1574, Diederik van Sonoy, the governor and friend of William of Orange, built a defence here to hold back the Spanish troops of Philip II during the eighty-year war (1568-1648). The shipbuilding industry in this area was famous not just in the Netherlands but also far afield. In 1697, the Russian Tsar Peter the Great came here incognito for a few years to learn the shipbuilding trade. The house where he lived can be visited. In recognition, Tsar Peter put the colours of the Dutch flag into the Russian one, although in a different order. In the new Russia, where the precommunist flag has been reinstated, you can see these colours once more. In the 1950s, an initiative was taken to save the 17th and 18th houses, other buildings and windmills. They were taken apart stone for stone and built up again in what is now the Zaanse Schans. All the houses here are lived in. You will find Albert Heyn's first grocery shop here, as well as various museums, a clogmaker, a cheesemaker and a centre for old crafts and trades. Of the original 600 windmills from this area, six have been preserved. The first mill to be built here was a sawmill (1592). Sometimes several of the old windmills were restored into one new mill. On this page the green mill 'De Kat', a working mustard mill dating from 1786, the black 'Gekroonde Poelenburg', a sawmill from 1869, and the 'De Zoeker', an oil mill from 1672. The grain mill 'De Bleeke Dood' can be seen on the next page, top left.

KLOMPENMAKERIJ

REDERIJ DE SCHANS
RONDVAARTEN
REDERIJ
DE SCHANS
RONDVAARTEN
PRICE

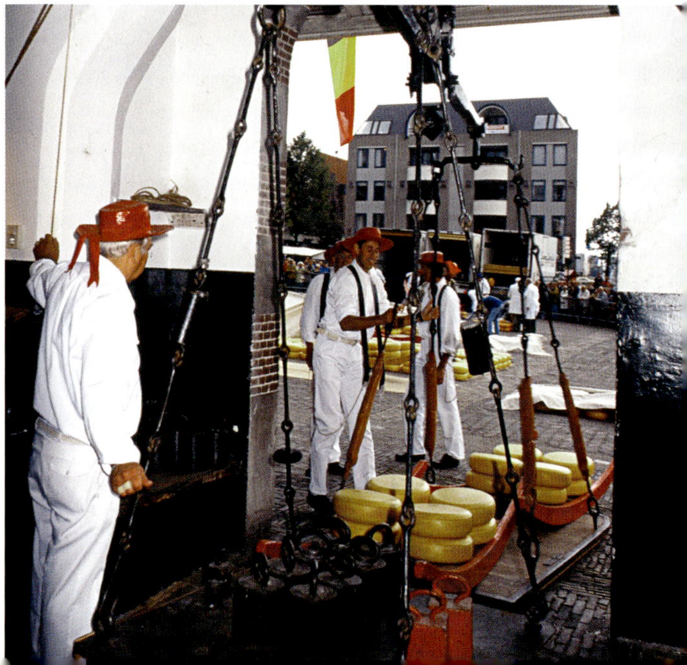

It was in **Alkmaar** that victory began. Dutch children learn this at school and it refers to the 16,000 Spanish besiegers who withdrew in 1573, during the eighty-year war (1568-1648). The autumn rains and muddy conditions were too much for them. The Spanish troops were led by Federico of Toledo, the son of the much-feared Count of Alva. Left, the magnificent weighing house (Waag), which was originally built in the 14th century as a chapel to the Holy Ghost, but was converted into a weighing house in 1582. The tower of the Oude Kerk in Amsterdam was used as a model for this building (see page 10). The Tourist Information Office and Dutch Cheese Museum are now housed here. In the summer a traditional cheese market is held here every Friday, at 10 am. The cheese is inspected to check its quality, weighed in the weighing house and cheese carriers then take it to the lorries for transport. During market hours, vehicles are not allowed into the town centre. There is a special car park from which a bus service will take you to the market. A few kilometres to the north of Alkmaar lies **Broek op Langedijk**. Of interest here is the Broeker Veiling museum. This vegetable auction dates from 1887. The farmland is directly bordered by canals. Their primary function is water regulation, especially drainage, but the canals were also used for transporting the crops in flat-bottomed boats. The boats went straight to the auction, where they sailed past the buyers so they could buy directly from them. The old auction clock dating from 1903 is still in working order. This clock shows the price, and by pressing a button you decide what you are prepared to pay.

From the 9th century onwards, many little towns, such as Monnickendam, Edam, Hoorn, Enkhuizen and Medemblik, were built up along the coast of what was then the Zuider Sea. These towns flourished because of the merchant shipping on the Zuider Sea and were very important until the 18th century. When the dam was closed in 1932, the Zuider Sea was transformed into a lake, the IJsselmeer.
On the left **Hoorn**, which has not lost its old character. Jan Pieterszoon Coen (1587-1629), governor-general of the Dutch Colonial Empire in Indonesia, was born in this town. You can see his statue in front of the Waag (weighing house). The photos also show Hoorn's main tower, dating from 1532. It is situated in the port, which is now only used as marina.
Upper right, **Edam**, which is world famous for its cheese. The photo shows the narrow Kwakelbrug, a bridge just wide enough for one person, and the bell tower in the background.
Enkhuizen with its impressive Drommedaris, which used to be part of the 16th century city walls. The tower has a carillon, which is the work of the Hemony brothers and is considered by many to be the most beautiful in the Netherlands. A cafe can now be found in this building.
Well worth a visit is the Zuider Sea Museum: it has an indoor part with, among other attractions, some old wooden ships, and a part outside (lower right photo). The panorama photo of the Zuiderspui, middle right, shows the back of the houses with their wooden porches and charming little gardens.

Bergen, also called Bergen-Binnen, lies to the west of Alkmaar, and is much loved by artists. The ruins of the church, destroyed in 1574 by the Spanish, are worth visiting. **Bergen aan Zee** is a popular coastal resort. Upper right, you can see the famous 32 km long and 90 m wide IJsselmeer dam. The closing ceremony was performed by Queen Wilhelmina on 28 May 1932. Some 15 million m^3 clay and 27 million kg sand were used for its construction. The dam runs from the province of Noord Holland to Friesland. In the 60 years following its construction, the dam transformed the old dangerous Zuider Sea into the new, safe IJsselmeer. The Noord-Oostpolder and the 12th province of the Netherlands, Flevoland, were created and some 250,000 people now live in this reclaimed land. The **Wadden Islands** lie in the northernmost part of the Netherlands. On the North Sea side they have beautiful sandy beaches and dunes, while on the other side you will find little fishing villages. During the summer, many tourists visit the islands by boat, for instance from Den Helder to Texel, from Harlingen to Vlieland and Terschelling, from Holwerd to Ameland and from Lauwersoog to Schiermonnikoog. The photo shows the largest island, **Texel**, which is 24 km long and 9 km wide. By ferry, it takes 20 minutes to reach the mainland. Oosterend is one of Texel's quaint villages. The lighthouse is in the north, near Cocksdorp. On the panorama photo, you can see the Slufter, a characteristic landscape on the seaside of the dunes, where seawater and fresh water are constantly being mixed. The result is remarkable vegetation and a breeding ground for hundreds of different types of birds.

Haarlem is the county town of the province of Noord Holland. The late gothic Grote Kerk (St. Bavo's) was built between 1370 and 1520. The interior of this church is beautiful, with its world-famous Müller organ dating from 1738. In 1766, the 10-year-old Mozart played on this 5000-pipe organ. The painter Frans Hals and writer Bilderdijk are buried at St. Bavo's. The entrance for visitors is at the side of the church: 23 Oude Groenmarkt. Upper right photo; the Corrie ten Boomhuis at 19 Barteljorisstraat. The 13th century town hall on the Grote Markt (photos below) was originally a hunting lodge. Fires repeatedly destroyed the complex, such as in 1573 during the 80-year war. In 1799, it was bought by the state for 25,000 guilders. In 1804 the city bought it back again, paying for it with four paintings. The statue of the inventor of the Dutch art of printing, Laurens Jansz Coster, also stands on this square, photos below.

LET OP!

Ten Boom
MUSEUM

Spring is the season of flowers. The huge bulb fields cover large areas of land with an incredible carpet of gorgeous colours. This breathtaking scenery can be best admired at the **Keukenhof**, an international exhibition covering 70 acres with 6 million tulips, narcissus, daffodils, hyacinths and other flower bulbs, ancient trees, flowering shrubs, splendid ponds, fountains and many statues.

Culemborg

Gouda brings to mind cheese, stroopwafels (syrup wafers) and candles. Dating from 1450, its gothic town hall, the oldest in the Netherlands, dominates the imposing triangular square. The south facade is flanked by little towers and the steps at the main entrance are decorated by many statues. The Waag (weighing house), which dates from 1668, lies on the same square and has a bas relief on the face of the building showing cheese being weighed. Not on the photos, but certainly worth a visit, is the 13th century St. Janskerk. The church is much visited for its matchless stained glass windows by the Crabeth brothers. **Leiden** has been a university city since 1575, and its scholars include Arminius, Gomaris, Boerhave and Descartes. In the 16th and 17th century, the city was a place of refuge for protestants from Flanders, France and England. It is the birthplace of the painter Rembrandt van Rijn (1606), the son of a miller who lived close to the River Rhine, to which he owes his name. The town hall, originally from around 1600, was rebuilt after a fire in 1929. Built in 1743, the corn mill, the Valk, (upper right) has seven storeys and up to 1964, ten generations of millers lived there. The mill is now a museum. The area around Galgenwater and the Morschpoort is still romantic, but the fact that Leiden has moved with the times is clear when you look at the new railway station. There is an express bus service from this station to the Keukenhof.

Erfgoedwinkel

The Hague, the seat of the Dutch government, is the country's diplomatic centre and the capital of the province of Zuid-Holland. The Hague is often mistaken for the capital of the Netherlands, but this has been Amsterdam since 1813. Here you can see the Queen in her gilded coach arriving at Ridderzaal (Knights' Hall) where, following tradition, she opens the parliamentary year. This is a beautiful and solemn occasion that takes place annually on the third Tuesday of September. The Queen comes out of the Noordeinde Palace (Beatrix's working quarters) in her gilded coach, and after a short ride she arrives at the Ridderzaal, which is located in the Binnenhof (inner court). On both sides of the Ridderzaal you can see the Houses of Parliament, which were used as such until 1992. These buildings date from around 1230. In the Binnenhof, opposite the Ridderzaal, you will also find a splendid fountain, built in neo-gothic style. Petra's little souvenir shop is close by. Photo below left, the Buitenhof (outer court) with its statue of King William II, and in the background the Gevangenpoort museum, with among other things a collection of instruments of torture. The orange pennants attached to the flags are the symbols of the close ties and love between the Royal Family and the people. On the photo far right you can see the Netherlands' first covered shopping arcade, The Passage, which dates from 1885 and was restored to its full glory in 1991.

INDUS
HORLOGES
ARCADE

Residentie Orkest
DR. ANTON PHILIPSZAAL

The Hofvijver (court lake), panorama photo below, and the government buildings are beautifully lit up on summer evenings. The prime minister has his office in the eight-sided tower. The small island in the middle of the lake has been a breeding place for storks for many years. The stork is also depicted on The Hague's coat of arms. On the other side of the Hofvijver, you will find the main embassies. The Mauritshuis, upper right, was built in the 17th century by Prince Johan Maurits of Nassau. It is now a museum and although quite small, it houses some very important works of art, including paintings by the Flemish school: Rubens, Rembrandt, Vermeer, Frans Hals, Averkamp and Jacob van Ruysdael. The concert hall showing the Dr Anton Philip's Hall, which was completed in 1987 and has a capacity of 1900 seats, is the base of the Residence Orchestra and is situated directly behind the new town hall.

In the miniature town of **Madurodam** in The Hague even the smallest people feel like giants. Everything around you is reproduced to 1/25 of its real size. Madurodam is a sort of synthesis of the Netherlands with many characteristic places such as the canals of Amsterdam, Alkmaar's cheese market, the windmills of Kinderdijk, Utrecht's Domtower, Rotterdam's Erasmus Bridge and its port with a burning tanker being extinguished. Too much to mention, you should go and see for yourselves. Right-hand page: **Scheveningen**. Since 1818 the original fishing village has grown into the biggest seaside resort in the Netherlands, a conglomeration of luxurious flats, hotels, restaurants. Below: the old fishing port on flag day. From this harbour, several shipping companies organise fishing trips at sea. Middle: the new Van der Valk restaurant on the 381 m long pier. Above: the Netherland's biggest ever sandcastle, built by INAXI on Scheveningen beach.

Upper left, a view of Scheveningen's beach and promenade from the front of the restaurant on the pier. Lower left, Noordeinde Palace, where Queen Beatrix works. It is situated in a rather ordinary street in the centre of The Hague, called Noordeinde. This building, dating from the 16th century and built by order of Frederik Hendrik, used to be known as the Oude Hof (Old Palace). In front of the palace there is an equestrian status of William the Silent of Nassau (1533-1584), who was also the Prince of Orange from 1538. Later he was to be known as the Father of the Fatherland. His fourth wife and widow, Louise de Coligny, lived here. Upper right, the Vredespaleis (Peace Palace) which was opened on 28 August 1913, just one year before the start of the First World War. In 1922 it became the permanent international court of arbitration. Since 1946, it is the International Court of Justice. Lower right, Prins Clausplein to the east of The Hague, the biggest traffic intersection in the Netherlands.

nuovo

Delft has a magnificent mediaeval town hall with a tower dating from 1300, the upper part of which is in gothic style from the 15th century. The tower was made part of the town hall, which was built in 1620 by Hendrik de Keyser. Opposite the town hall you can see the Nieuwe Kerk (St. Ursula's), an imposing gothic church from 1384. Its belfry is the second highest in the Netherlands. The tombs of the Dutch Royal Family are in this church, as well as that of Prince William of Orange. In the Grote Markt, the large market square opposite the Nieuwe Kerk, you can see the statue of Hugo Grotius (1583-1645), a talented Dutchman being a lawyer, diplomat, philosopher and poet. Lower left, the Oude Kerk (St. Hippolytus), founded in 1250. In this church, it is easy to follow the development of the gothic style. Inside there is a carved wooden pulpit from 1548. Upper right, the Prinsenhof Museum, which used to be the residence of Prince William of Orange, ancestor of the Dutch Royal Family. William of Orange led the Netherlands in its struggle against the Spanish occupation (1568-1648) and was murdered here on 10 July. Art and antique exhibitions are held in this museum and the famous Prinsenhof concert takes place here every year. Lower right, the Oostpoort, which dates from 1400, is part of a mediaeval defence fortress and it is the only remaining tower from the original eight. Delft is, however, best known for its pottery 'Delfts Blue' from the 'Porceleyne Fles' (Porcelain Bottle). This skilled handwork has been produced since 1500.

C&A

Rotterdam, as a city, has literally risen from its ashes following the devastation of its centre by bombing during the start of World War II. The Coolsingel is shown here with the town hall (1914-1920), one of the few buildings to survive the German bombing of 14 May 1940. Opposite the town hall, on Lijnbaan, you will find Mari Andriessen's monument (1957) for those killed in action between 1940-1945. Photo lower left, Beursplein with Naum Gabo's work of art 'The reconstruction' dating from 1957. Upper right, Beurstraverse (1966), which was designed by Pi de Bruyn. The oval green building in the background is the 23-storey World Trade Centre. Lower right photo, various facets of the Hofplein and Weena with the Millennium Building. The city with the largest freight port in the world owes its name to the little river the Rotte, which was dammed up in the 13th century: the dam on the Rotte became Rotterdam. Due to the construction of the 18 km long New Waterway (1866-1872, Pieter Caland), the city gained an open connection with the North Sea, which proved to be a decisive factor in the city's economic development. Nowadays it is one of the most modern cities in the Netherlands. Rotterdam is the city of huge docks, commerce, hardworking people, and modern architecture. 'Amsterdam has it' is the slogan of the inhabitants of the capital, and 'Rotterdam already had it a long time ago' is the answer of the inhabitants of this city.

Rotterdam's greatest landmark is without doubt the Euromast. In 1960, the first part was built with its platform and restaurant at 100 m. In 1970, it was extended to 185 m when the spectacular space tower was added. A lift constructed around the tower spirals up to the top. On the photo you can see the red lift halfway up the building. This unusual lift will take 32 people. In clear weather, you can see as far as 40 km. Lower right, the view to the east, from the platform at 104 m. Erasmus Bridge (by Ben van Berkel), 800 m long, 30 m wide with a 139 m-high pylon. This bridge, known to the Rotterdammers as the Swan, was put into use in 1996. The bridge connects the present city centre with the Kop van Zuid. The magnificent cruise ship the Rotterdam, middle photo, moored at the Cruise Terminal, Holland-Amerikakade.

CAFE
ROTTERDAM
Amsterdam

HOLLAND-AMERIKA LIJN

Amsterdam

In 1991 a start was made with the development of a new district on the left bank of the River Maas. This area is known as the Kop van Zuid. The World Port Center is located here, on the Holland-Amerikakade. After the Second World War, this was the departure point for Dutch people emigrating to Canada, Australia and the USA. In those days, we thought the Netherlands was full. It is now a mooring place for huge cruise ships. The photo shows the Amsterdam moored here in Rotterdam. What used to be the HAL (Holland-America Line), next to the World Port Center, is now the striking Hotel New York. Lower left, the Erasmusbrug, this time seen from the other (right) bank of the Maas. Lower right, the new Willemsbrug (1981), which replaced the old bridge of the same name. The part of the old bridge that can be raised to let ships pass through, the lifting bridge, remains as a monument, top right. In the background, seen from the middle of the old bridge, the new Erasmusbrug. Middle right, Rotterdam's Witte Huis. This white building, eleven storeys high, was build between 1897 and 1898 and was the Netherlands' first 'skyscraper'.

CAFE PLAN-C
Marlboro
Marlboro
Marlboro
Marlboro
Marlboro

BREEVEENTIEN

Near the Oude Haven (old harbour), you can see an example of Piet Blom's singular architecture, the cubic houses (1978-1984). These fanciful houses are built over the Blaak, one of the city's busiest streets, and connect up with the central library and an apartment
complex, which the locals call 'the pencil'. One of the cubic houses is open to the public. The former light ship, the Breevertien, lies in the Wijnhaven, near the Maritime Museum. The monument 'Devastated City' by Ossip Zadkine represents a desperate man without a heart, after the bombing of the centre of Rotterdam on 14 May 1940. Lower right, the River Nieuwe Maas from the Erasmus Bridge with the new touring boat, the Abel Tasman at embarkation quay of the Spido. The red bridge in the background is the Willemsbrug dating from 1981.

Delfshaven, photo left, used to be the harbour of Delft. It is one of the oldest parts of the city. Many buildings have been restored making this a quarter full of character. The pilgrim fathers left from the Oude Kerk (Old Church) here in 1620 with the Mayflower on their way to America. Close by, you will find the Dubbele Palmboom museum and the 'Zakkendragershuisje'. The view from the Euromast looks in the direction of Hoek van Holland, across Delfshaven. The corn mill was originally used to grind grain for the gin distillery. One of Rotterdam's great scholars was Erasmus (1469-1536). The right-hand page shows his statue in front of the Grotekerk (St. Laurens). Rotterdam University is named after him. The Grotekerk, dating from 1646, was destroyed during the three days of heavy bombing in May 1940 before the country surrendered to the Germans. A view from the World Trade Building in an easterly direction with the Grotekerk to the left, the cubic houses of Piet Blom in the middle and Willemsbrug to the right. Lower right photos: left, the offices of the insurance company 'Nationale Nederlanden'; its towers are 93 and 150 m high. Directly opposite, right, the 149 meter high Millennium Building. The first 14 storeys house the five-star hotel 'Westin Rotterdam', while the top 20 floors are filled with offices.

The Netherlands is the land of clogs, tulips and windmills. There used to be as many as 3000 windmills in the country and these days some 1,000 remain. Mills can be classified into two groups according to their function: polder draining mills and industrial mills. The purpose of polder mills was to drain water from the reclaimed land. Originally, various mechanical methods were developed to achieve this, such as treadmills, water mills and windmills, but by the start of this century only the windmills remained in use. Industrial mills were built for such activities as grinding grain to make bread (or gin as in Schiedam), sawing tree trunks into planks or pressing oil. There are various different types of windmills, such as tower mills that were set on a pedestal so that surrounding buildings did not impede the wind, and smock mills with a revolving top to catch more wind. The majority of polder mills in the Netherlands are of the polder mill type. The red mill, upper left, dating from 1830, can be found in **Maarssen** near Utrecht and is a smock mill. This same mill is also shown on the cover of this book. Well worth visiting are the windmills at **Kinderdijk**. These polder mills were built from 1740 and most were in use until 1950. The white mill, left, can be found in **Enspijk** near Deil and is used for grinding grain to make bread. The yellow mill, lower middle photo, the St. Hubertus Mill dating from 1801 is situated in **Kelmond** in the province of Limburg. This is the oldest type of windmill. Lower right, at the **Zaanse Schans**, a mill from 1869, which is used to saw tree trunks.

The rivers Noord and Lek converge close to the villages of **Kinderdijk** and Albasserdam in the province of Zuid Holland. Kinderdijk is especially well known for its 19 windmills, dating from around 1740. Not only are there more windmills here than anywhere else in the Netherlands, but they are also the biggest, and thought to be the most impressive. The vanes are up to 29 metres long. They were in use up until 1950, pumping water from the polder grounds below sea level. These days, electrical pumping machines are used for this purpose. Without the sand dunes along the North Sea coast and the dykes, half of the Netherlands would be under water. These days the windmills are not only kept in good working order for the tourist industry, but also so they can immediately be put into use again in case of an emergency. From the inviting 'Molenhoek' cafe, you can take a tour by boat past the mills. The second windmill from the cafe is open to the public.

Schoonhoven, with upper right the 15th century town hall, is a charming town at the spot where the little River Vlist joins the much larger River Lek. This place used to be a centre for goldsmiths and silversmiths. **Oudewater** is especially famous for its witches' weighing house, the Heksenwaag. During the centuries, the scales were used by merchants to weigh their goods. The inhabitants of Oudewater, well known for their honesty, used to weigh many people accused of witchcraft and give them a certificate to prove that they weighed enough not to be a witch. That saved a lot of lives because if they were too light, they were accused of practising witchcraft. You can still get yourself weighed here and receive a certificate of your weight. Photos below, from right to left: **Vianen**, a mediaeval little town at the point where the River Lek joins the Merwedekanaal. **IJsselstein**, with its grain mill the 'Windotter' dating from 1732.

A beautiful area of meadows, irrigation canals and willow trees, called Lopikerwaard, flanks the west of the province of Utrecht. This area between IJsselstijn and Oudewater has been described in a fascinating way by Herman de Man, who was born in Woerden in 1898. He knew the area better than anyone. The little river the Lange **Linschoten** meanders whimsically through this pretty area. Linschoten, upper left photo, is a romantic village. The Hollandse IJssel also flows through this same area and it was on this river that the little town of **Montfoort** was built in 1170. It is sited halfway between Gouda and Utrecht. The lower left photo shows the back of the 15th century town hall, with its old turn bridge and bridgemaster's house. Montfoort also has an old castle that was destroyed by the French in 1672. A luxury restaurant is now located in this castle. What is also worth a visit but not shown on the photos is the Commanderije, the temporary residence of the Knights of St. John, which dates from 1544. Located on the Hofstraat, this building has been completed restored.

Various views along the River Lek between Schoonhoven and Vianen. Upper left photo, a little house built against the dyke, on the landside. Both photos below show a view over the part outside the dyke, thus on the riverside. Sunset over the river from the bridge at Vianen.

Utrecht is the fourth city in the Netherlands and it is also one of the oldest. The Romans constructed the first fortress (Castellum) here in the year 48 AD. The canals were built between the 12th and 14th centuries. In olden times, the wharves were used for unloading ship's cargoes. The goods were carried to warehouses in the basements, connected with the houses in the neighbourhood. Nowadays these wharves are very popular on account of the numerous cafes and the basements have been turned into attractive restaurants. The 112 m high Domtoren is the highest church tower in the Netherlands, and visitors can climb the 465 steps to the top. Lower left photo, the Paushuize, a house built for Pope Adranus VI (1459-1523). It was not completed until after his death. He was the only Dutch pope, although he never actually visited Rome. Right, from top to bottom: **Rhenen** on the River Nederrijn with the tower of Cunera Church, which was built between 1492-1531, completely destroyed in 1945, and then rebuilt to its original state. There was heavy resistance here against Germany's dominance during the fighting in May 1940. **Wijk bij Duurstede** on the River Lek with the 'Rijn and Lek' windmill. What is unusual here is that you can drive under the mill. This mill is thought to have been used as model by the painter Ruysdael. Just outside this little town, you will find the ruins of Duurstede Castle. Finally **Zeist** with its famous castle, the Slot Zeist, which was built between 1677 and 1686.

The photos to the left, going clockwise, show the following: The River Vecht, which flows from the city of Utrecht northwards, to enter the IJmeer at Muiden. The Dutch tend to visit **Muiden Castle** (upper left photo) at least twice in their lives, once on a school trip and once with their grandchildren. The castle was originally built in 1204 by the Bishop of Utrecht and later extended by Count Floris V, the first 'socialist' aristocrat, who was murdered for this reason in 1296. From 1621, it became a centre for intellectuals and linguists, including P.C. Hooft, Vondel, Tesschelschade, Roemer Visser and Constantijn Huygens. The locks at **Mijnden** provide watersporters a connection between the River Vecht and Loosdrecht Lakes. Along the River Vecht you will find many beautiful country houses, such as Rupelmonde shown here, which used to be the summer residence of wealthy merchants from Amsterdam. To the west of the Vecht, Haar Castle at **Haarzuilens** (panorama photo), which was rebuilt in 1892 in its original 14th century style. In 1672, the French under Louis XIV destroyed the castle. The castle is open to the public. In **Breukelen** the 17th century Nijenrode Castle can be found (lower right), which is now used as an institute of education: the University of Nijenrode, as it is called, is a famous international business school. **Loenen** is a charming village on the Vecht with a very fine looking old drawbridge. Also in the direct vicinity is the green smock mill, the Trouwe Wachter, in **Tienhoven**.

LEEUWENBURG

Nederhorst den Berg, a little village in Noord-Holland close to the border with the province of Utrecht, with top left its 13th century castle, Nederhorst. It is a splendid castle with four six-sided corner towers. The restoration of this building was nearly completed when a disastrous fire totally destroyed it in 1971. Work started again and two years later it was restored to its original style. Situated close by is the Dutch Reformed church with its 12th century Romanesque tower. In 1551 an extension was added and remedial work was carried out in 1892. Back in the province of Utrecht, the Loenderveense windmill, just outside the village of Loenen, is located in a water-collection area for Amsterdam. Off to Noord Holland again, we find **Hilversum**, the radio and television centre of the Netherlands. The town hall, below left, was built between 1928 and 1932 by W.M. Dudok (1884-1974). The cubic shapes of varying sizes were well ahead of their time. **Weesp**, in Noord-Holland on the border of the province of Utrecht, with its town hall and municipal museum from 1776, below middle. On the right-hand page we return to **Utrecht** with a view of the Dom tower from the Zadelstraat. This is the Netherlands' highest tower, built in gothic style between 1321 and 1382. Below right, the pavement cafes on the wharf of the Oudegracht just past the Ganzenmarkt and the old town hall. The Oudegracht runs from one end of the city to the other and has many bridges. Originally, the canal joined the River Rijn to the Vecht.

Aarlanderveen

Maarssen

Marken

The province of Zeeland has a great deal to offer the tourist - history but also the latest in modern technology. **Middelburg**, right-hand page, is the provincial capital. The beautiful gothic town hall dominates the market square, where a market is held every Thursday. It was in 1452 that Flemish architects, inspired by Brussels' town hall, started construction. The town hall was destroyed in the early days of the war in May 1940. The Abbey is an extensive monastery complex, founded by St. Norbertus in the 12th century and now housing the Zeeland Museum. The 14th century tower Lange Jan (Long John) is part of the Abbey complex. It is well worth climbing for its magnificent view. Charming 18th century houses line the Rotterdamsekaai, Rouaansekaai and Londensekaai. The names refer to former unloading quays of ships and where they came from. The middle photo below shows the shooting range, built between 1607-1611, originally for the rifle association, but later it was converted into a military hospital. The car ferry between Vlissingen and Breskens was in use for 137 years, until a new tunnel to Zeeland Flanders was completed in 2003. Vlissingen is the birthplace of the famous admiral Michiel de Ruyter (1607-1676). To this day, he is honoured in Hungary because he freed dozens of protestant Hungarian clergymen who were galley slaves on Turkish ships. As early as the 14th century, **Vlissingen** was important because of the trade with England. The esplanade is lined with hotels offering fascinating views of shipping on its way to Antwerp. On the other side of the Westerschelde lies Zeeland Flanders, which borders Belgium. In **Hulst** you will find the beautiful St. Willibrordusbasiliek.

BAKKERIJ
WARME BAKKER

Also in the province of Zeeland is **Zierikzee**, left, with its Zuidhavenpoort, seen here in the direction of the town. The square tower has a carillon in the dome, dating from the 15th century. The drawbridge inside the town walls links up the Zuidhavenpoort to the Noordhavenpoort. The 14th century town hall has a richly decorated wooden spire, upper left photos. The town hall is now a museum dedicated to the town's history. Lower left, the Nobelpoort, a square town gate with two high, narrow towers. The 5 km long Zeeland Bridge is one of the longest in Europe. Upper right photo shows the little harbour of the delightful town of **Veere**. After the floods of 1953, when nearly 2000 people lost their lives, the Delta Works were constructed and made operational. All the main distributaries, except for Westerschelde, can be closed in the event of high waters in extreme conditions. The **Oosterscheldekering**, middle right photo, which was built between 1976 and 1987, is the jewel in the crown of these works. The photo shows one third of the Delta Works, sometimes called the eighth wonder of the world. Its total length is 2800 meters and it is made up of 65 pillars, each 42 meters in width, with 62 moveable steel bolts and built from 18,000 tons of cement. A permanent exposition, Delta Expo, has been set up on what used to be the artificial island 'Neeltje Jans'. A gigantic replica provides an overview of the total works.

Dordrecht. This city forms an important junction for shipping on account of its position on three rivers, the Beneden Merwede, the Noord and the Nieuwe Maas. In the old part of the city, colourful quays, canals and old gables are still intact. From here, you can take a boat trip to the Biesbosch. Left, the interior of the 15th century Grote Kerk. Due to subsidence, the slanting tower was never completed. It can be climbed via 279 steps. Between 1618-1619, the protestant National Synod of Dordrecht was held in this church and it is still of historical importance today. All the protestant churches, except for the Remonstrants, joined together here. **Breda**, right, was chosen as Nassau's residence in 1404. From the Grote Markt you have a lovely view of the Grote Kerk (Our Lady's). The 97 m high tower has a carillon with 49 bells. The impressive tomb of Engelbracht II of Nassau (1451-1504) is found here, and it is also the burial place of Anna van Buren, the first wife of William of Orange. The Spanjaardsgat (Spanish Gap) is a passage through the water in the old fortifications of the city. In 1590, Prince Maurits used a peat barge as a 'Trojan Horse' to smuggle his solders into the city and oust the Spanish troops. Breda Castle has housed the Royal Military Academy since 1828.

Limburg is the southernmost province of the Netherlands, both geographically and as far as temperament is concerned. It used to be of great economic importance to the country because of its mining industry. Nowadays the chemical industry is expanding in Limburg, and tourism is also becoming an increasingly valuable activity. The beautiful rolling countryside gives even Dutch tourists the feeling of being abroad. **Maastricht** is the provincial capital and the oldest city in the Netherlands. Its original Roman name is 'Mosae Trajectus' (crossing over the Maas). On the left-hand page, Onze Lieve Vrouwebasiliek, dating from around the year 1000. On the main photo, right: the Vrijthof, with St. Servaasbasiliek (right) and St. Janskerk (left). The only American military cemetery in the Netherlands is in **Margraten**, lower middle photo. Some 8302 soldiers who gave their lives for our freedom are buried here. The cemetery has been in use since November 1944 but was not completed until 1960. In the museum, the military operations of the liberating allied armies are illustrated on enormous marble walls. The road to Margraten was first built in the first century AD by the Romans. Later, this same road was used by Napoleon, then by Hilter in 1940 and by the allied troops in 1944.

Hoensbroek Castle, also in Limburg, is without a doubt one of the finest castles in the Netherlands. It stands on three islands, each surrounded by a moat. The oldest parts date from the 13th century. Until 1927 the house was owned by the noble Hoen von und zu Hoensbroek family. However, they left the castle in 1787 to settle in the German town of Geldern. The walls of the round towers are three metres thick. From 1928 to 1943 extensive remedial work was carried out to save the castle from ruin. It is now in use as a cultural centre and a restaurant. In Zuid Limburg you will find fine examples of half-timbered houses in the Epen, Mheer, Noorbeek areas, and here on the main photo, in the surroundings of **Mechelen**, along the little rivers the Lomberg and the Mechelder. On the photo on the right, you can see the River Geul as it meanders from Valkenburg on the Geul, here close to Wijlre, towards Wittem. The marl landscape is exposed in some places in the south of Limburg because of erosion, as can be seen in the photo below left, taken near **Bemelen**. From this village, an hour's walk from Maastricht, you have a lovely view of the city to the west.

Valkenburg aan de Geul, in the south of Limburg, is a popular tourist centre. The main photo shows the castle ruins, dating from 1040, which dominate the town. Two gates remain from the original town walls, the 14th century Grendelpoort and the Berkelpoort from the 15th century. This area is well known for its caves, which form a 70 km long underground network. You can visit an old coal mine. **Roermond**, with its beautiful Munsterkerk (Our Lady's) dating from the 13th century can be seen in the top right photo. It is a showpiece of late Romanesque style from the Rhineland area. The church was restored between 1863-1890 by the well-known architect P.J.H. Cuypers. Lower right, **Venlo**, situated in a central position in Limburg, with its town hall from 1597. Octagonal towers flank the face of the building. **Vaals**, lower middle, with the Boudewijn tower on Belgian soil near the 'Drielandenpunt' (321.5 m). This is the point where Germany, Belgium and the Netherlands meet. **Thorn**, a white village 14 km southwest of Roermond, lies close to the Belgian border. The Stiftskerk was originally part of a cloister for women. A museum for religious art is now housed in this church. Close by, you will find the Wijngaard square, the paving of which is decorated with geometrical figures. Under the influence of the French revolution in 1794, there came an end to the independence of this small area. The charm of this village is undoubtedly its white 18th century houses.

's-Hertogenbosch, to the left, is the provincial capital of Noord-Brabant. One of the most beautiful religious edifices in the Netherlands is the Sint-Janskathedraal, which was built between 1380 and 1530 in a Brabant gothic style. Between 1629 and 1810, this church was used for protestant services. Then Napoleon gave the church back to the Roman Catholics. Since 1929, it has the status of cathedral. **Nijmegen** was conquered by the Romans under Caesar Augustus and burned to the ground in the year 70 AC. The bridge over the River Waal was retaken from the Germans by the allied troops on 20 September 1944; this in contrast to the 'Bridge too far' in Arnhem. The Grote Markt, with in the middle of this square the Waag (weighing house) that dates from 1612 and was built in a renaissance style. The red and black shutters produce an unusual colour effect against the dark red background. There is a restaurant on the ground floor of this building. **Eindhoven**, also known as the city of lights. In 1891 the family firm of Philips was founded. This firm originally only produced light bulbs, hence the name. The saucer-shaped Philips Competence Centre, the Evoluon, was opened in 1966. The mediaeval castle of **Helmond** houses the Municipal Museum. In **Overloon** the National Military and Resistance Museum can be found in a 14 ha park. Here you can see war material from the allied forces and the Germans, including tanks, planes, a V-1, a one-man submarine and many authentic documents and photos.

Arnhem, the capital of the province of Gelderland, lies on the River Nederrijn just past where it branches from the IJssel. The city is particularly well known for one of the most tragic events in the history of the liberation of the Netherlands during World War II: the battle of Arnhem of September 1944. This piece of history, referred to under the code name 'Market Garden' became widely known because of the film 'A bridge too far'. On 17 September 1944 more than 10,000 British parachutists landed near **Oosterbeek**, some 10 km to the west of Arnhem. The British were ordered to secure the bridge of Arnhem, lower left photo, for the advancing American troops. Partly because important information was not taken seriously in London, the operation turned into a nightmare. Oosterbeek, the Airborne Cemetery, lower right, the last resting place of 1667 British and 79 Polish solders. The Airborne Museum stands on the site where the leader of the operation, General Urquhart, had his headquarters: Huize Hartestein, 232, Utrechtseweg. **Apeldoorn**, a city in the heart of the Veluwe, owes its fame to the museum Paleis Het Loo, upper left photo. The summer residence of the royal family since 1686, this palace was opened to the public in 1984 as a museum. Its interior exhibits permanent and temporary collections. The stalls house many historical royal carriages. The complex is surrounded by extensive wooded parkland.

On the left-hand page, you can see the east of the province of Overijssel. Beautiful farmhouses grace the area of **Ootmarsum**. The photo below shows the farmhouse 'Los Hoes', which is a museum. Here you can see how people used to live together with their animals in one area. Not far from here, in **Singraven**, you will find Singraven Castle, the little river, the Dinkel, and a 15th century windmill. This mill still saws wood and grinds coffee. Right next to it, there is a restaurant and outdoor cafe, with a view of the mill. **Enschede** is the biggest town in the province of Overijssel. On the photo left, a protestant church, originally dating from 1200, with a Romanesque tower. On the page to the right, the surroundings of **'s-Heerenbergh**, to the east of Arnhem. The impressive castle, Huis Bergh, originally dating from the 13th century dominates the whole area. One of its famous residents was Willem van den Bergh, an aristocrat from Gelderland who married William of Orange's sister in 1556. This family joined forces with the Spanish enemy to fight against their own country. The tower mill is in **Zeddam**, which is close by.

On the left, the new station in **Amersfoort**, which dates from 1998. The city was granted a charter in 1259. Parts of the old city walls, which date from the 13th century, are still intact. The painter Mondriaan was born here in 1872. Just 12 km to the north lies the old fishing village of **Spakenburg** with its little harbour on the Eemmeer. Some of the women here still wear traditional costumes, especially on the 'Spakenburgse days', the last two Wednesdays in July and the first two in August. Top right, the new railway stations of **Almere** and **Lelystad**, both towns in the new Flevopolders. The development of Almere started in 1975 and it is expected to grow to a population of 150,000 inhabitants. It has a marina on the Gooimeer. Panorama photo right, the old steam-driven pumping station 'Hertog Reijnout' in the Arkemheem polder in **Nijkerk**. The pumping station is in a bird sanctuary on the lake between the former coast and the empoldered land in the south of Flevoland. It is an unusual industrial monument from the 19th century. Since 1994, it has a visitor's centre. The pumping station is sometimes operational, but it is also open to the public when it is not working. **Harderwijk** was a Hanseatic town on the Zuider Sea. A few quaint little alleyways and parts of the town walls with the Vispoort (fishing gate) still remain, below right. Thanks to its location on what is now the Veluwemeer, its beach and two marinas, Harderwijk attracts many tourists. The surrounding countryside, the Veluwe, is characterised by nature reserves of woods, heather and sand drifts.

Almere Centraal Station

Schokland used to be an island and now lies in the Noord-Oostpolder. Reclaimed from the sea in 1942, this polder is part of Flevoland, the twelfth province of the Netherlands. In contrast to the former island Urk (see next page), Schokland lies in the middle of dry land. What used to be the harbour is now drained, see main photo, and looks out over land. Schokland has been on the UNESCO's list of cultural treasures since 1995. From 1300, **Elburg**, lower left photos, developed into a lively little port on the former Zuider Sea. This little old town has retained its mediaeval character. From the 14th century square towers of the Nicolaaskerk you have a splendid view of the patterns in the pavements that are paved with black and white pebble stones. **Kampen**, in the province of Overijssel, is sited on the banks of the River IJssel, close to the Ketelmeer. The beautiful gate, the Cellebroederspoort, used to be part of the 15th century city walls. In the foreground the handsome little statue of Pallieter, the hero of the book of the same name (1916) by Felix Timmermans. Below right, view over the IJssel of the old town with the tower of the town hall, dating from 1543, to the left.

Lelystad is the county town of the new province of Flevoland, the twelfth Dutch province. The province consists entirely of polders, which have been reclaimed from what used to be the Zuider Sea, and since 1932 the IJsselmeer. The name Lelystad comes from the engineer Lely, the father of the Zuider Sea works. At the Batavia shipyard in Lelystad, replicas of ships from the Golden Age are built as part of an unemployment project. Young people are given the opportunity to gain two years of valuable experience. Between 1985 and 1995, work was carried out on a replica of the VOC ship the 'Batavia'. The ship is 56.6 m long and 10.5 m wide with a sail surface area of 1180 m^2. The original Batavia, carrying 341 passengers, sank on its maiden voyage off the west coast of Australia. Since 1995, work is being done on another reconstruction, namely that of the 'Seven Provinces'. The ship will probably be completed in 2005. The shipyard, which is also a museum, is on the Oostvaardersdijk and is open daily from 10 to 17 hours. On the page to the right, the former island of **Urk**, now part of the northeast polder. In 1939 the dyke from Urk to Lemmer was completed, so that Urk was no longer an island. Urk remains a lovely fishing village on the IJsselmeer. The inhabitants form a close community and regard Sunday as a day of rest. The fishermen's monument is in memory of the fishermen lost at sea. All their names are written on a wall.

SL11

Zwolle, the county town of the province of Overijssel. On the upper left photo you can see the beautiful Thorbecke-gracht with its 15th century tower. The birthplace of the liberal statesman Thorbecke is at no. 11. Photo middle left: the remains of the Sassenpoort, part of the mediaeval town defences. This town gate from 1409 has two corner turrets, rounded in shape but becoming octagonal at the top. The Sassenpoort now serves as the Public Records Office. Lower left: **Hattem**, an old fortified town in the province of Gelderland. Right-hand page, photo upper right: **Deventer**, delightfully situated on the IJssel. The Gelderse IJssel, one of the largest rivers in the Netherlands, meanders through the lovely country-side to its estuary in the IJsselmeer. Deventer dates back to the time of Charles the Great. The city joined the Hanseatic League and became a centre of trade, science and religion. Great names as Geert Grote (1340-84), Jacob Revius (1586-1658) and Sweelinck (1562-1621) still live on in the Netherlands. The Grote Kerk (St. Lebuinus) originally dates from 1040, but was reno-vated in 1459 by Hendrick de Keyser. The tower, which can be climbed, has one of the largest Hemony carillons in the Netherlands. On the other side of the IJssel, an impres-sive bulwark windmill dating from 1863 dominates the landscape. At Olst and Wijhe, you can take a ferry across the IJssel. Attractive farm-houses have been built on the fertile land behind the dykes of the IJssel.

Giethoorn, upper right photos is known as the Venice of the Netherlands. Many of the houses have been built on islets, and you can only reach them on foot, by little wooden bridges. The province of Drente is known for, among other things, its megalithic tombs. These are prehistoric burial places constructed of enormous stones. Of the 53 megalithic tombs in the Netherlands, all but one can be found in this province. Herds of sheep, as here in **Ruinen**, are also a feature of this area. In the grounds of the former concentration camp, **Westerbork**, 14 radiotelescopes are set up, each with a diameter of 25 m. The monument is built up of 102,000 stones on what used to be the muster square. There is one stone for every Jew, gypsy or resistance worker deported to Germany from here between 1942 and 1945, never to return. Every Tuesday, 93 times in total, a goods train left with victims for Auschwitz and Sobibor. Only 5000 of those deported survived the war. The province of Overijssel with **Staphorst**, upper left, a village that stretches over 10 km. Beautiful farmhouses lie along the main street, with doors and window frames painted bright green or blue.

Groningen, capital of the province of the same name, has been a university town since 1614. This is one of the reasons why it is such a lively place. The tower of the Martinikerk stands high above the city and can be seen from afar. The 13th century basilica was rebuilt in the 15th century in a gothic style. The charming square, the Martinikerkhof, invites the students to relax and take a break while on the other side you can enjoy a beer at De Kosterij. The hall of the main railway station was restored to its original style, that of Isaäc Gosschalk from 1895, in 1999. Directly opposite the station, you will find the multiform Groningen museum (1992-1994). Several different architects contributed towards the building of this museum, including Alessandro Mendini (1931), Michele de Lucchi (1951) and Phillipe Stark (1949). In **Noordpolderzijl**, in the salt marshes outside the dykes, there is a small harbour for shrimp fisherman. This area also has many beautiful farmhouses, such as in Uithuizen.
In a northeasterly direction from this town, a route 120 km long runs past 12th and 13th century villages. Some of them are built on mounds. The photo shows the Reformed Church of **Kantens**, which was built in the 12th century. The natural gas that has been extracted in this province since 1960 will be of great economic importance in the 21st century. Large amounts are found in, for instance, Slochteren.
The new Eems power station in Eemshaven has been producing electricity from natural gas since 1976.

MARLENA
USQUERT

Top left, still in the far north of the province of Groningen, sunset over the Reitdiep near **Zoutkamp**, seen in the direction of Lauwerszee. Below left, in the south east of the province, close to the German border, the old fortified border town of **Bourtange** with its entrance gates. Dating from 1593, this little town has been restored as a museum village to its state in 1742. On the right-hand page and the following pages we become acquainted with the province of Friesland, the only part of the Netherlands to have its own language. Top middle photo shows **Bolsward** with its renaissance town hall (1614-1717). Witmarsum, where Menno Simons, the founder of the Anabaptists was born, is close by. **Stavoren** with its statue of the proud widow of the famous legend, looking out to sea against the background of the old white drawbridge. A parade of skûtsjes (flat-bottomed boats) is always a fascinating sight. **Hindelopen** (in Frisian Hynljippen) is a small town with a magnificent little church. Five airmen from the Allied Forces of World War Two are buried in this churchyard, some of them unknown.

HB
KL

The province of Friesland is in summer much loved by water sporters. Photos to the upper left, going clockwise from the top, show the provincial capital **Leeuwarden**, (in the Frisian language: Ljouwert) with the Waag (weighing house) dating from 1598. Butter and cheese used to be weighed here until 1884. The city is also the birthplace of the dancer and mysterious double spy, Mata Hari. The smallest of the eleven Frisian towns, **Sloten** (in Frisian: Sleat), was granted a charter in 1250. The photo shows the area around the Lemsterpoort with one of the remaining town walls, near the corn mill. A view from the bridge in **Woudsend**. In the friendly little town of **Dokkum**, the British missionary Bonifatius and 52 of his companions were murdered in the year 754. But you mustn't hold the present inhabitants responsible for this event. Partly built on a mound, this town was actually on the coast in the 17th century and was then very important for its trade and shipping. Lower left, **Harlingen**, the only seaport in Friesland, was the homeport of the whalers who sailed to Greenland until about 1850. These days, ferries take tourists to the Wadden Islands: Vlieland and Terschelling. A walk through the old streets and along the old quays of Harlingen is certainly worthwhile. The charming little town of **Hindelopen** with its narrow canals and little wooden bridges is situated on the IJsselmeer. It enjoys fame through its traditional costumes and furniture. In the very inviting museum of the Hidde Nijland Foundation, a large collection of traditional tools and costumes are exhibited.

Since 1909, on the rare occasions that the winter is very severe, the 'Elfstedentocht' is held in Friesland. It is absolutely essential that the canals are covered by at least 15 cm of ice before this unique race on skates can take place. Sometimes, ten years can go by before the conditions are right again. The race is over a distance of 210 km through eleven towns. Anyone not arriving at the finish within seven hours is disqualified. The top left photo shows **Sneek**, with its lovely water gate, dating from 1613, at the entrance of the harbour. The photo on the left was taken two days before the race was held. The ice was then thick enough for a car to drive on it. The car clears a track through the snow for the skaters. On the photo to the right, the same water gate taken from the same place, but this time in the summer as yachts are sailing through it. Lower right, **Sloten** in the winter with skaters on the ice. On the previous page, top right, the same bridge, this time taken from the other side and in the summer with yachts on the water. Lower left photo, near **IJlst**, where a boot is frozen into the ice.

Kromme Rij

The rivers Noord and Lek converge close to the villages of **Kinderdijk** and Albasserdam in the province of Zuid Holland. Kinderdijk is especially well known for its 19 windmills, dating from around 1740. Not only are there more windmills here than anywhere else in the Netherlands, but they are also the biggest, and thought to be the most impressive. The vanes are up to 29 metres long. They were in use up until 1950, pumping water from the polder grounds below sea level. These days, electrical pumping machines are used for this purpose.

Woudsend, Friesland

Without the sand dunes along the North Sea coast and the dykes, half of the Netherlands would be under water. These days the windmills are not only kept in good working order for the tourist industry, but also so they can immediately be put into use again in case of an emergency. From the inviting 'Molenhoek' cafe, you can take a tour by boat past the mills. The second windmill from the cafe is open to the public.